THE STORY

THERE IS A TEVYE!...

He may not be the milkman, and he may not look like Topol, but somewhere in your community, wherever you live, there is a Tevye, the character played by Topol in the film of *Fiddler on the Roof*.

It does not matter whether your village is a towering apartment block in the middle of a concrete jungle or a collection of huts in the African bush; somewhere, there is Tevye, a man who stands out from all the rest.

The remarkable thing about Tevye is that though he stems from Jewish folklore and the tales of Sholom Aleichem, the famous Yiddish writer, his appeal is both immediate and universal.

As a stage musical, *Fiddler on the Roof* has been seen by 30,000,000 people throughout the world, and everywhere its sincerity and humanity have been instantly recognized. In Tokyo, the Japanese actor who played Tevye declared, "We know why it is a success here, but how is it they like it in America?"

Topol, the Israeli actor who made a name for himself in the London stage production, says, "The genius of Sholom Aleichem was that he used the background of Jewish folklore and humor as a frame to see the general problems of a father, a husband, a member of a minority group. All the problems and experiences that are meaningful to Tevye are universal ones."

Fiddler on the Roof is the story of a small Jewish village in the Russian Ukraine in the time of the Tzars, where ordinary people live, making the best of a not very encouraging set of circumstances.

Those who saw the musical play recognized it easily. The village and the people could be anywhere in the world.

The millions who go to see it will identify at once: Yente, the busybody matchmaker; Motel, the honest tailor; Lazar Wolf, the butcher and the richest man around; Perchik, the revolutionary student; and Tevye, the milkman with five daughters. They are friends and neighbors of the world.

TRADITION

Words by SHELDON HARNICK
Music by JERRY BOCK

FIDDLER ON THE ROOF

Words by SHELDON HARNICK
Music by JERRY BOCK

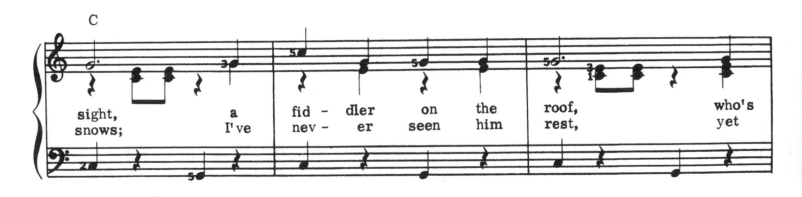

Why should he pick so cu-ri-ous a place to play his lit-tle fid-dler's

tune? A fid-dler on the roof, a

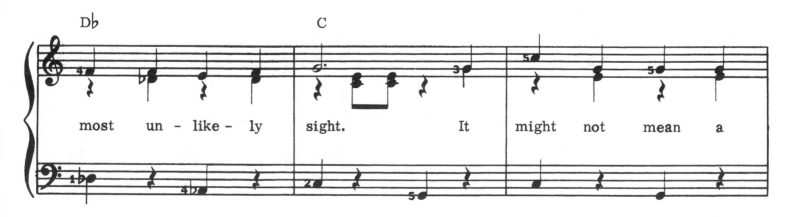

most un-like-ly sight. It might not mean a

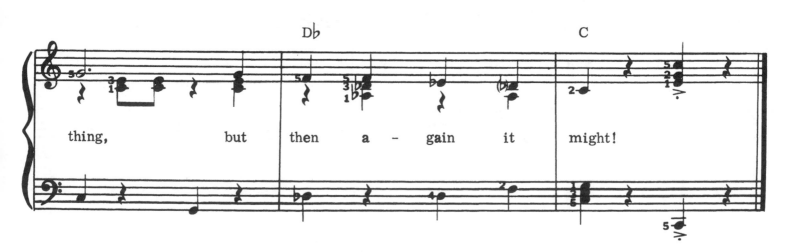

thing, but then a-gain it might!

SABBATH PRAYER

Words by SHELDON HARNICK
Music by JERRY BOCK

May the Lord pro-tect and de - fend you, may he al-ways shield you from shame;
May you be like Ruth and like Es - ther, may you be de - serv-ing of praise;

may you come to be in Par - a - dise a shin - ing name.
strength-en them, O Lord, and keep them from the stran - ger's ways.

May God bless you and grant you long lives.
(May the Lord ful - fill our Sab - bath

IF I WERE A RICH MAN

Words by SHELDON HARNICK
Music by JERRY BOCK

FAR FROM THE HOME I LOVE

Words by SHELDON HARNICK
Music by JERRY BOCK

MIRACLE OF MIRACLES

Words by SHELDON HARNICK
Music by JERRY BOCK

SUNRISE, SUNSET

Words by SHELDON HARNICK
Music by JERRY BOCK

2. Now is the little boy bridegroom,
   Now is the little girl a bride.
   Under a canopy I see them, side by side.
   Place the gold ring around her finger,
   Share the sweet wine and break the glass;
   Soon the full circle will have come to pass.
   (To Chorus:)

MATCHMAKER

Words by SHELDON HARNICK
Music by JERRY BOCK

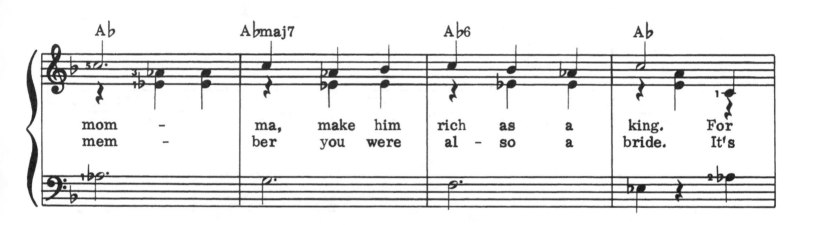

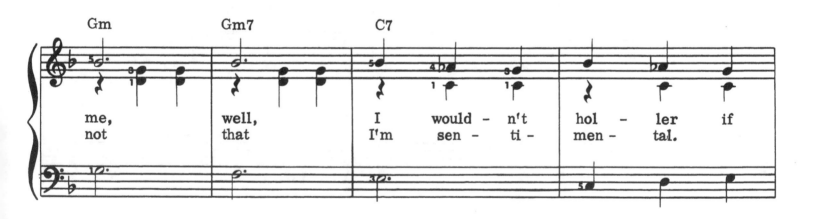

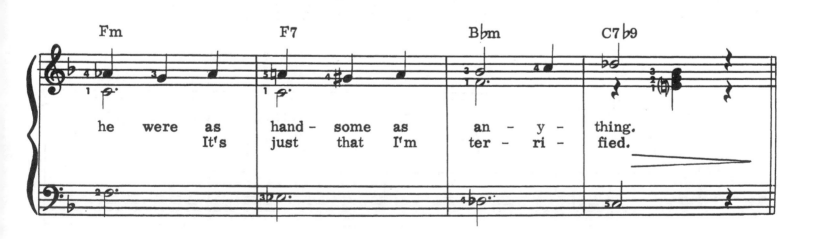

TO LIFE

Words by SHELDON HARNICK
Music by JERRY BOCK